Email Archiving FOR DUMMIES®

by Bob Spurzem and
Bill Tolson

BICENTENNIAL
1807
WILEY
2007
BICENTENNIAL

Wiley Publishing, Inc.

Email Archiving For Dummies®

Published by
Wiley Publishing, Inc.
111 River Street
Hoboken, NJ 07030-5774

Copyright © 2008 by Wiley Publishing, Inc., Indianapolis, Indiana

Published by Wiley Publishing, Inc., Indianapolis, Indiana

For general information on our other products and services, please contact our Customer Care Department within the U.S. at 800-762-2974, outside the U.S. at 317-572-3993, or fax 317-572-4002.

ISBN: 978-0-470-24993-2

Manufactured in the United States of America

10 9 8 7 6 5 4 3

Contents at a Glance

Publisher's Acknowledgments

We're proud of this book; please send us your comments through our online registration form located at www.dummies.com/register/. For details on how to create a custom For Dummies book for your business or organization, contact bizdev@wiley.com. For information about licensing the For Dummies brand for products or services, contact BrandedRights&Licenses@Wiley.com.

Some of the people who helped bring this book to market include the following:

Acquisitions, Editorial, and Media Development

Project Editor: Jennifer Bingham

Editorial Manager: Rev Mengle

Business Development Representative: Karen Hattan

Cartoons: Rich Tennant, www.the5htwave.com

Composition Services

Project Coordinator: Kristie Rees

Layout and Graphics: Claudia Bell, Carl Byers, Carrie A. Cesavice, Stephanie D. Jumper, Melanee Prendergast

Proofreaders: Laura Albert, John Greenough

Publishing and Editorial for Technology Dummies

    Richard Swadley, Vice President and Executive Group Publisher

    Andy Cummings, Vice President and Publisher

    Mary Bednarek, Executive Director, Acquisitions

    Mary C. Corder, Editorial Director

Publishing for Consumer Dummies

    Diane Graves Steele, Vice President and Publisher

    Joyce Pepple, Acquisitions Director

    Kristin A. Cocks, Product Development Director

Publishing for Travel Dummies

    Michael Spring, Vice President and Publisher

    Kelly Regan, Editorial Director

Composition Services

    Gerry Fahey, Vice President of Production Services

    Debbie Stailey, Director of Composition Services

Table of Contents

Foreword

What's in That Email and Why Does It Matter?

by Laura Dubois
Research Director, Storage Software
IDC

● ●

*T*oday's businesses are focused on managing valuable information while at the same time mitigating potential risk from it. Corporate information needs to be protected from compromise, retained according to regulatory requirements, and be available in the event of audits or legal discovery or for general business use. The pervasiveness of email in today's corporate environment to communicate and conduct business continues to fuel email growth. However, today's businesses must be able to manage email growth while satisfying requirements for email availability, retention, and content-oriented retrieval. Content-oriented retrieval is of particular relevance in regulatory audits or electronic discovery, in which emails associated with a particular keyword or relevant to a specific topic are frequently sought. Email archiving applications and solutions address both of these technical and business requirements.

Email archiving applications provide an automated and efficient way of storing, indexing, and retrieving individual email messages and file attachments in real time by individual users, IT staff, and other authorized parties from both inside and outside the firm. Email archiving differs from backup and retrieval solutions in that the latter are designed only to provide regularly scheduled copies of an email server or disk. Backup and retrieval solutions enable email to be brought back up and running after an email server or disk fails, but these solutions don't maintain copies of emails exchanged between backups, retain copies of emails deleted by users after the backup is replaced with a newer one, or move email content off primary email servers to more efficient storage systems. Today's email archiving applications, on the other hand, are designed to handle these tasks, and can be delivered as an on-premises software solution, preinstalled on an appliance, or as a hosted service.

According to IDC, the email archiving applications market was a $477 million market in 2006, realizing 45 percent growth over 2005. The email archiving applications market continues to be fueled by litigation and electronic discovery, regulatory requirements for record retention, as well as overall mailbox management. In comparison, the overall IT industry has been hovering around 5 percent growth year over year. The phenomenal growth of email archiving applications is driven by electronic discovery, in particular by amendments to the Federal Rules of Civil Procedure, regulatory compliance, and the overall need for storage and email application performance optimization.

Because email users tend to express themselves in an informal manner, and because metadata is associated with email, these communications are often sought during the discovery phase of corporate litigation. Email archiving solutions can help companies more quickly find relevant email and reduce the cost of electronic discovery. Regulations in different industries may stipulate that related content contained in electronic records be retained for specified time periods or outline rules to secure the privacy, security, and lack of compromise to sensitive information. Email archiving supports records retention requirements and also enables content indexing for easy search and retrieval of relevant messages and attachments based on audit requests. In addition, email archiving can be used to manage mailbox size by regularly archiving older or infrequently accessed data. Archiving saves space by moving messages from the email server into an archive repository, thus improving performance while giving users access to their archived email.

Email is a core component of business communications today, and firms need to ensure that they have adequate controls in place to protect, retain, and preserve relevant email content. With the volume of email increasing annually, firms also need to find a way to manage growth with relatively flat budgets and limited IT administration. Today's email archiving applications provide a solution to meet these legal, regulatory, and business needs. Through email archiving, companies have an automated and efficient way to store, index, and retrieve individual email messages and file attachments by individual users, IT staff, and other authorized parties.

Introduction

The growth in email for business and personal use has been nothing short of phenomenal. Compared to the telephone, email needed only a short period (from the early 1990s to the present) to become the number one form of business communication. According to the Radicati Group, storage requirements will grow from almost 18 megabytes per user per day in 2007, to over 28 megabytes per user per day in 2011.

Email's popularity is impacting your business in many ways. The huge volume of email is making it increasingly difficult to store and keep accessible for end-users. End-users struggle with mailbox quotas and spend precious hours each week managing mailbox capacity. New laws and regulations are requiring access to historical email — email that is difficult to retrieve from backup tapes.

No wonder you're concerned about better management for your email application! And you're not alone. In all organizations, email management is considered critical to the success of the business, and the content contained in email is considered part of the company's intellectual property and a record of business.

About This Book

Email Archiving For Dummies is designed to help you better manage your email application servers by introducing an enterprise application called *email archiving*. Email archiving works in conjunction with your email servers to improve how you manage email.

- ✔ Email archiving manages old email in its archive thereby reducing storage costs on the email server.

- ✔ Users access archived email as easily as regular email allowing them to keep years of email at their fingertips.

- ✔ Legal and compliance officers can access historical email in the archive quickly for litigation and compliance.

These are just a few of the ways that email archiving can help you regain control of your email application servers.

If you care about preserving your valuable email data and making sure you're ready for whatever comes down the pike, this book is for you. No matter what your background or title, this book helps you understand the problems you're facing managing email and how email archiving can help.

Looking at Email Applications

Email applications are available from many manufacturers, including Microsoft, IBM, and Novell just to name a few. The Microsoft email server brand is called Exchange Server, and its desktop email client is branded Outlook. IBM's email application is called Domino Server and its email client is called Notes. Novell's email application is called GroupWise. The list of email applications is long, but these are some of the most popular solutions deployed in organizations.

In this book, we focus on Microsoft Exchange Server. Exchange Server is the market leading enterprise email application and it is supported by the leading email archiving solutions. The issues discussed also apply to other email applications.

How This Book Is Organized

This book is organized into three main parts, each with a specific focus.

Part 1: Getting to Know Email Archiving

You may be surprised that email archiving exists to help your email server run better in so many ways. In this first part, we explain in plain language the challenges you face managing email and how email archiving can help. We explain how an email archiving system functions, how it captures email from the email server, and how it stores the email in the archive.

Part II: Getting to Know Search, Retention, and eDiscovery

Management of email for legal discovery and compliance is critical for every organization. In this part, we give you a basic understanding of eDiscovery and how it relates to email. We review the important new Federal Rules of Civil Procedure (FRCP) and discuss how it impacts email retention and disposition. Wrongful handling of email can possibly result in legal fines and penalties, so you will want to pay close attention to this part. We also explain how to do various kinds of searches.

Part III: The Part of Tens

No *For Dummies* book is really a *For Dummies* book without the part of tens. In this part, we include a chapter with some important questions to ask when shopping for email archiving. Next, we provide a list of the top ten benefits of email archiving. You will also find a useful appendix.

Icons Used in This Book

In the margins of this book, you can find some icons to help guide you through the content.

The tip icon gives you a little guidance on ways to use what you just read. The text gives you knowledge, and the tip gives you a little nudge in the right direction.

Ever wish you had a little voice that lets you know when something could go wrong and tells you what to avoid? This icon is probably the closest thing you're going to get.

This tip marks information that's very important. Get your pencil and notebook out and write this down so you can remember it!

Where to Go from Here

Email Archiving For Dummies is organized so that you can take it home, put on your favorite listening music, and read it like a novel, or you can keep it at your desk at work and flip through it to find areas of particular interest. Whether you're new to managing email or an old pro, you will find information in this book to make your email server hum along like a well-oiled machine.

Part I

Getting to Know Email Archiving

It's an e-mail from my mother. She wants me to know how happy she is for us.

In this part . . .

This is the main meat of the book in which we introduce you to email archiving and explain the main problems it addresses. We also pull back the covers, so to speak, and share with you the internal working of an email archiving system. Now, don't be afraid, we don't overwhelm you with lots of technical jargon. Using the information we will provide, you will be ready to interact positively with email archiving vendors.

Chapter 1

Email Archiving Basics

● ●

In This Chapter

▶ Understanding basic email archiving systems

▶ Choosing between in-house and hosted solutions

▶ Understanding the storage benefits of email archiving

▶ Looking at the benefits of email recovery with email archiving

▶ Discovering how email archiving increases user productivity

● ●

*T*he term "archive" doesn't conjure long, stuffy halls full of banker boxes and papers anymore. Even something as seemingly nebulous as email can be archived, indexed, and ready to produce on short notice. An *email archiving* system is simply a stand-alone application that works with your email server to help you manage email. For example, email archiving captures and preserves all email traffic flowing in and out of the email server. It processes the email data and stores it on magnetic disk storage. When the need arises to search historical email for internal investigations or for a court-ordered legal discovery, you can search thousands of email records in seconds by using search tools embedded in the email archiving system.

Getting to Know Email Archiving Systems

So, you think you may need an email archiving system. You may be surprised how many of the challenges you face in managing your email server can be greatly improved with the help of email archiving. For years, administrators have turned to email archiving to solve their most pressing email problems.

Take the quiz in the sidebar "A quick quiz" to see whether you need an archiving system. However, we suspect that you may already know that you need a system since you picked up this book.

Email archiving can help solve some of the most challenging problems facing your organization with regard to email management. Email users send and receive hundreds of emails each day and demand unlimited mailbox capacity and fingertip access to years' worth of email.

Email archiving solutions can improve email storage efficiency by removing email and attachments from the messaging server based on administrator-defined storage policies, while preserving access to end-users.

For litigation support and internal investigations, email archiving solutions allow compliance and legal officers to easily search email stored in the archive and avoid the costly exercise of searching backup tapes.

A quick quiz

A pop quiz on the first day? Don't panic. This is easy. To help you understand if the challenges you face in managing email can be addressed by email archiving, answer *true* or *false* to the following statements:

✔ Users are constantly asking for more mailbox capacity.

✔ HR is calling you to search email and you're in a panic.

✔ A major law suit is pending and email records are part of it.

✔ Your email server is full and you need to add five new employees.

✔ Industry regulations require that you preserve email for five years.

✔ Email is being lost in local PST files.

✔ Attachment files are filling your email server.

✔ Your email server just plain runs slow!

If you said *true* to any of these questions, you have an email management challenge. The more often you said *true,* the bigger the challenge. In fact, we expect that you answered *true* to just about all of these questions. That's the bad news. The good news is that help is out there.

For compliance with federal and state regulations, email archiving solutions store email according to managed retention policies. When retention periods expire, email is automatically deleted by the archiving solution.

Looking at the Different Types of Solutions

Two types of email archiving solutions exist: in-house and hosted. In this section, we look at each.

When comparing in-house versus hosted email archiving, determine how many mailboxes you wish to archive and for what length of time. Then get a quote for each. Now you can quickly compare the total costs of each solution.

In-house solutions

In-house email archiving solutions are installed on a dedicated server (or servers) in the same data center as the email server(s). The email archiving server accesses the email server locally for data capture and users access the email archive using their email client via the existing company network. Sensitive corporate data is kept and controlled by your employees in your facility.

The archived email can be searched as many times as needed for discovery. In-house email archival solutions are customizable and are available from multiple vendors to support the leading email applications. Email archiving software is typically licensed by the number of mailboxes and additional fees apply for support and maintenance. Long-term costs can be noticeably lower than hosted solutions.

Hosted solutions

Hosted email archiving solutions are an option for customers who don't wish to install their own email archiving solutions in-house for whatever reason. For what's usually a monthly fee, a number of mailboxes can be archived off-site with no on-site setup required. Because the email is captured while in transit, all email applications are supported. With a hosted

A look back

Believe it or not, email archiving systems have been around for a long time. In fact, they've been around since the early days of email. The first email archiving solutions appeared in the mid-1990s, and their purpose was to reduce storage demand on the email server. Beginning in 2002, the demand for email archiving exploded in the financial services industry when the Securities and Exchange Commission required that all of its members archive email. Today, new generations of email archiving solutions are appearing driven by the demands of legal discovery and regulatory compliance.

email archiving solution, you need not worry about managing the email archival servers and you can access archived email via a Web-based search application provided by the hosted service provider. This solution usually has lower start-up costs, but service costs can be high over the long-term. Refer to Chapter 7 for more detail.

Reducing Email Storage Loads

Just as nature abhors a vacuum, email users seem to abhor an empty email box. Back when mailbox quotas were 10 megabytes, they filled quickly. As email attachments became more prevalent and email quotas increased to compensate, they still filled quickly. Now, quotas are measured in hundreds of megabytes, and still users cry for more. Users will always find ways to fill up their mailboxes.

To reduce the amount of email data on the email application server, email archival solutions remove email and attachments using policies based on the age and size — it is that simple. Once the email is removed it is replaced with a small *stub file* (or shortcut) and it is stored safely in the archive.

Users access archived email in the same manner they access normal email, which is to "double-click" the shortcut in the email client. The email and attachments in the archive can also be searched for legal discovery and compliance.

Too much stubbing can slow down Microsoft Outlook so be careful. In situations where tens-of-thousands of email messages are being considered for stubbing, simply moving the email to the archive without stubbing is the better choice.

Recovering Lost Email

Admit it, you've deleted an email and wished to have it back either a moment or a few days later. You can ask friends to forward you a copy of the email, or you can try using an email system's built-in recovery tool. If your system and your friends fail you, then email archiving can help.

Restoration of email from the archive is a feature that all email archival solutions can perform. After all, what kind of useful archive won't let you look at your stored information? Depending on the email archival solution you're using, administrators search the archive and restore individual messages, or end-users search their archived mailboxes themselves and restore individual messages. It is a relief to know that the email archives can recover email that otherwise may never be found.

 When comparing email archival solutions ask for a "live" demo so you can see for yourself how easy it is to search and browse the archive and restore individual email.

Helping End-Users

Limitations aren't good for business. When users are limited by mailbox capacity, they're forced to spend valuable hours deleting email and/or moving email to offline storage files. Both activities take time, and users may accidentally delete or overwrite valuable information. Archiving helps your end-users by giving them the location to store years' worth of email; email that might otherwise have been deleted due to lack of space on the email server.

Archiving makes it easy for end-users and administrators to find old messages (either their own or others) and retrieve that information at any time. Using search tools provided by the email archiving solution, you search using names, dates, and wildcards to find what you need quickly, without having to search manually through years' worth of emails. Well done!

Chapter 2

Processing Email for Archival

*I*magine looking under the hood of a modern automobile. It may seem complicated at first glance, especially given all the technology present in today's cars. This chapter lifts the hood on email, showing you how it works and how it's powered.

Looking at Data Capture Basics

A core function of email archiving is email data capture. Email originates on email servers and travels over the company network and the Internet to reach destinations across the world. Given the mind-boggling number of possible addresses and routes, it's amazing that emails reach their destinations at all. It ranks as one of the wonders of the world (along with the triple cheeseburger and the defense of the 70s-era Pittsburgh Steelers). Email archival solutions *read* (copy) individual emails and attachments and store them in the archive. Email is most commonly captured at its source on the email server. However, it is also possible to capture email in transit, usually at a junction point in the company network.

Examining Exchange Data Capture

Microsoft Exchange is one of the market leading enterprise email applications. Every email archival solution faces the same challenge when supporting Exchange: how to capture data continuously without impacting Exchange. In this section we review two traditional methods and one new method that email archival solutions use to archive email directly from Exchange.

Don't fold the MAPI wrong!

MAPI, or the Microsoft Application Programming Interface, allows the Outlook client to communicate with the Exchange Server. First generation email archival solutions use MAPI to read email in Exchange, making copies to archive. MAPI runs on a schedule (for example, weekly) and archives messages that are too old or too large to usefully remain in Exchange. MAPI is useful to reduce storage on the Exchange Server.

Writing in your journal

For continuous data capture of Exchange email for legal discovery and compliance, Exchange *journaling* is used. Journaling is a feature of Exchange that holds a copy of all incoming and outgoing email in a journaling mailbox. Email archiving solutions access the journaling mailbox, using MAPI, to read and store email in the archive. In this manner, a copy of email is saved in the archive and serves as a record of important email conversations for legal discovery and compliance.

Log shipping

A new method of data capture for email archiving is *log shipping*. Log shipping relies on the Exchange Transaction Log Files as a source of email information. Exchange Transaction Log Files, or "log files" for short, go beyond journaling to capture *all* email information being added or deleted to the Exchange Mailbox Stores. The log file contents are saved in the archive and serve as the most comprehensive record of all mailbox information for legal discovery and compliance.

 If your Exchange Server is running at full capacity, the performance burden of journaling may be too much for it to handle. Consider log shipping as an alternative. It places no performance burden on Exchange.

Eying Archival Policies Basics

Archival policies allow you to manage exactly what email is archived and how long it stays in the archive. This policy control is an essential difference between the email archive and the email server. You see, end-users control the email server. End-users decide when to create email, when to send it, and when to delete it. The email archive, on the other hand, is managed by policies set centrally by the administrator. Are you getting the feeling that email archiving gives you the power to manage everyone's email? In a certain way of thinking, you're correct!

Archival policies determine which mailboxes are archived, and if log shipping is used, they allow you to configure the class of email content (such as calendars, contacts, notes, and tasks) for archival. If certain email content (like personal mail, meeting reminders, and spam) isn't deemed a record of business, then it need not be archived. After email reaches the archive, another set of retention policies define how long the email remains.

Retention policies are specified in days, weeks, months, and years and usually correlate to a particular industry requirement. When email reaches the end of its retention period, it is automatically disposed. The only exception is if the retention policy was suspended as part of a litigation hold. For more on litigation holds, see Chapter 6.

Perusing PST Processing

Microsoft Exchange users can store email offline in PST files. A *PST file* is a personal folder file in Microsoft Outlook. PST stands for personal storage. PST files are stored on desktops, laptops, and file servers. These files make email more portable and shoulder some of the burden of email servers. If you travel frequently, you appreciate being able to open and read email even in a busy airport. However, you likely hate PST files with a burning intensity if you're the company lawyer. When litigation arises, as it's bound to do, you can't locate, access, or search for email that is scattered who-knows-where in PST files.

Email archival solutions commonly provide features that copy the contents of PST files into the email archive. Processing email from offline files isn't much different from processing email from the email server — email is email, so this is a natural fit for email archiving. After the offline email is processed, it can be searched quickly and easily along with all email. This ability to search PST files addresses the legal demands for better control of offline email. Users can keep their offline email files, but the trend is to destroy them after they're archived. It seems the legal requirements for email security outweigh the user benefits of offline email.

PST files can be disabled in newer versions of Exchange, but first find out if your email archival solution requires PST files in any way. Some do and this may interfere with your plans to eliminate PSTs.

Chapter 3

Storing Email in the Archive

· ·

In This Chapter

▶ Understanding single instance storage

▶ Deciding whether you need WORM disk or not

▶ Understanding the long-term storage implications for email archiving

· ·

*T*he internal workings of the email archive are important to understand. First, the knowledge will satisfy that growing concern you may have about where all of your email data is being stored. Second, you never know when it may come up in a bar trivia game. Email archiving solutions take many steps to help reduce the total archive storage. This chapter outlines each method and explains how it helps to reduce archive storage.

Single Instance Storage

Single instance storage (SIS) is a process that email archival solutions use to help reduce total archive storage. The basic process is simple — the archive stores only one copy of each original email and attachment. If one person sends an email and attachment to ten other people, that accounts for ten copies of the email in the email server. If you add in the times the same email is replied to or forwarded by the recipients, a single email can be duplicated hundreds of time. That's a lot of times for that list of jokes about mothers-in-law to make the rounds.

SIS can help reduce total archive storage by as much as 40 percent.

WORM Disks

WORM disk — sounds kind of weird! WORM is an acronym that stands for write-once-read-many and is commonly associated with optical media, CDs, DVDs, and magneto optical disks. So, are you wondering, "What does this have to do with email archiving?" Well, if your organization operates under the guidance of the Securities and Exchange Commission (SEC) then you may already know the answer. In the financial services industry, Rule 17a-4 specifies that all email transactions be stored on non-erasable and non-rewritable WORM storage. It is that simple!

The drawback of WORM storage is speed or cost. In the financial services industry, where WORM disks are required, you have no choice. But in all other industries, WORM disks are optional and not widely deployed.

Long-Term Archival

How long must email be kept in the archive? Well it depends. In the healthcare industry, email information that is part of the patient record must be retained for the life of the patient. In the financial services industry, email must be kept for up to seven years. Every industry is different.

Email archival solutions manage long-term email storage using admin-defined retention and disposition policies. Using the policies as a guide, email archival solutions store the email in the archive and protect it against unauthorized access or tampering. When the retention period expires, the email archival system disposes of the email record completely.

Look for email archival solutions that save a digital signature for each email. Years later, the archived email can be compared to its original signature to verify authenticity.

Part II

Getting to Know Search, Retention, and eDiscovery

The 5th Wave   By Rich Tennant

"I like getting complaint letters by e-mail. It's easier to delete than to shred."

In this part . . .

Do you like to read mystery novels? If you do, this part of the book is for you! In this part we dive into many of the important legal and discovery issues surrounding email. Are you aware that email is a record of business and can be subpoenaed in court along with other business records? Failure to produce email evidence can result in fines and penalties for your organization, so pay careful attention. In this part, we also discuss the important process of searching your email archive both for legal purposes and just so end-users can find emails they need.

Chapter 4

Finding Email in the Archive

● ●

In This Chapter

▶ Conducting the search of an email archive

▶ Understanding the benefits of end-user email searches

▶ Understanding the benefits of enterprise-wide email searches

● ●

*E*mail archiving solutions should offer two main functions when everything shakes out:

✔ The ability to capture email and other Exchange objects in a secure archive.

✔ The ability to quickly and easily find information within the archive.

Having both a quick and simple search capability for end-users and powerful comprehensive search capabilities for IT and legal are an absolute must for the solution to be useful. This chapter discusses both.

Enterprise-Wide Mailbox Searches

There will be occasions when you need to search across the entire email archive, usually for legally driven reasons like an eDiscovery order or for HR-related reasons like inappropriate use of the system, harassment, or suspected criminal activity. For these types of searches, you need access to and permissions for specific areas or the entire archive. This access is controlled centrally by the IT department.

The email archiving system should automatically keep access and audit records of who has accessed the archive as an administrator or auditor and exactly what material they accessed. This audit capability protects all parties from misuse of the archive.

A much more powerful search capability is in most cases provided by a special application that can access and search the archive. This search function is usually given as a client application to members of the legal department or members of the IT group. It should also provide other functionality like searches within searches, Boolean searches, saved searches, saved results sets, exporting results sets, workflow capability for assigning results sets to different auditors, tagging capability, and assigning litigation holds on specific content for eDiscovery requirements. (We look at legal eDiscovery requirements companies face today in Chapter 6.)

To be able to meet the intent of FRCP and eDiscovery requirements for a corporate email system, an email archiving solution with the previously mentioned advanced search capability would dramatically reduce the time required to search the email archive, the cost of responding to litigation, and the overall risk of not producing all responsive email.

Basic End-User Searches

We can confidently predict that one of the first uses you'll have for your new archive is finding an old email for an employee, whether it be for reuse, research, or even finding a forgotten phone number. Most email archiving solutions provide a way for an end-user to access archived messages. That is, if IT administrators have given employees access to the archive.

Some email archiving solutions provide a separate application that end-users need to kick off to access the mailbox archive. Other solutions allow the end-users to access the archived email directly from within the Microsoft Outlook client. Obviously it is easier for the end-users if they don't have to leave the Outlook interface and start up a separate application. But for either process, the basic search is the same.

End-user searches are usually based on some basic criteria, including the following:

- ✔ Keywords such as "2007 forecast" or "project ABC"
- ✔ The email address or name of either the sender or receiver, such as "Bill Tolson" or "Product Management"
- ✔ Domains like Mimosasystems.com or abanet.com
- ✔ The date and time the message was sent

You should be able to search on one or more of these criteria.

The email archive "Quick Search" screen in the end-user Outlook client provides a basic search form for searching for a word or phrase. That basic search of the end-user's mailbox archive can be quick and easy. In a sample case, the authors searched for the term "case study" and pressed the Search button. Twenty-nine emails were returned in 1.331 seconds and presented in the search results window.

The data in the search results window helps users narrow down exactly which email message they're looking for. For example, it includes information like what folder each specific email was found in, who sent the email, the complete subject line of each email, the size of the email (which indicates whether the email has an attachment), and who the email was sent to. The preview pane, below the search results window, shows a preview of each email message selected and lets users easily narrow down the search to the specific email the end-user was looking for. The end-user can also double-click the specific message and bring back the message in the standard email message window for reading, replying, forwarding, or even opening any attachment.

Be sure to install antivirus applications within your infrastructure to guard against malicious email viruses. Using the archive preview pane on an infected message is just as bad as opening it. Commercial virus protection software can eliminate this risk.

More Advanced Searches

The basic search functionality discussed in the preceding section doesn't always give you the results you're looking for. Sometimes a slightly more complicated search is required. To narrow a search more quickly, you need to include more search criteria.

You may need to consider the point in time at which the mailbox needs to be accessed — do you need to have access to the mailbox as it was six months ago, four months ago, two weeks ago, or yesterday? Being able to look at Exchange objects at different points in time can give you a bunch of interesting information — like when it was received, when it was deleted, what mailbox folders it resided in, and so on.

Another important criterion is what type of object you want to search for. Is the content in an email message or an associated attachment, or could the content be located in a calendar entry, a task list, or possibly embedded in contact information? Most email archiving solutions allow you to perform a search through their email messages, but few can archive and search through all the other objects in the Exchange mailbox.

Other search parameters to consider are the specific words or phrases you want to search on, the time frame to search through, and narrowing the search to only received emails, only sent emails, only modified emails, or some combination thereof.

Chapter 5

Retention and Disposition of Email in the Archive

In This Chapter

▶ Reviewing the basic requirements for an email retention policy

▶ Implementing the best strategies for retaining email in your archives

▶ Understanding the basics of email disposition

*E*lectronic storage isn't as costly as a physical warehouse, but you need to clean each one out eventually to make room for new records. It's just too expensive in time and money to keep everything. That's why it's important to decide what email will be archived and for how long it will be kept. The answers to these questions are the basis of this chapter.

Setting Guidelines

It is an accepted fact that corporate email includes business records or in certain circumstances, controlled records. *Controlled records* are usually records with privileged information like social security numbers or loan numbers, or those records that must be archived per government regulatory requirements. An email retention policy informs employees as to what email needs to be archived and for how long.

For an effective email retention policy, you need to distribute a written policy to all employees. This policy should include several of the topics shown below:

✔ **Effective Date:** This leaves no doubt as to whether the policy is currently in effect or is an old one that should be discarded.

✔ **Last change date and changes made:** This information confirms the policy's authenticity and appropriateness because regulations change over time.

✔ **Person or department responsible for the policy:** This gives employees or their managers someone to contact with questions.

✔ **Scope/Coverage:** This includes the geographic limits of the policy (if any), affected departments and offices, and a definition of what company information is covered.

✔ **Purpose of the Policy/Policy Statement:** This can include a company philosophy statement about the business/legal/regulatory reasons for records retention.

✔ **Definitions:** Defines what constitutes business records and applicable exceptions.

✔ **Responsibilities:**

- Business units/subsidiaries and special departments (such as the legal department)

- General employees

- Records retention coordinators

- Procedures for retention and deletion of email and attachments (if no automated email archiving system is employed)

- How the emails should be stored (usually in a PST)

- Where those PSTs should be stored, like a network storage target/share drive

- How often those files should be cleaned out

- How duplicate copies/convenience copies are treated

✔ **Consequences:** What happens if the policy isn't followed.

✔ **Appendix A:** Litigation Hold/Stop Destruction Policy, including a backup procedure.

✔ **Appendix B:** Current listing of department records retention coordinators and contact information.

A manually managed email retention policy relies on employees understanding and following the email retention policy. The obvious fact is that each employee will interpret the policy a little differently, so in reality you will have many different email retention policies. This fact is the main reason you need to adopt an email archiving solution.

Email Archiving Solution Policies

Most email archiving solutions allow you to set basic retention policies within the system. Most companies start out defining email retention policies based on their hardcopy retention schedule, which is a huge mistake. Hardcopy retention schedules are based on the content of each record. The expectation is that each employee is deciding on a record-by-record basis what specific business use the record reflects and, based on the retention schedule, how long it should be kept. However, most records in business these days are electronic, and an employee can generate hundreds a day.

An email retention policy should use high water marks. Using *high water marks* means that retention policies are based on department, accounting code, division, or geographic location (like another country with different retention laws). No email archiving solution has the ability to "decide" what any given email or attachment is about and then apply a specific retention period to it. Some of the better email archiving solutions will integrate with Microsoft's Active Directory, giving you the ability to set and keep retention policies current based on the employee's location, department, or accounting code.

Email retention policies are usually set centrally by the IT group and applied throughout the email system. Remember that policies can be set for the entire mailbox, or specific folders within the mailbox, such as Calendar, Deleted Items, Drafts, Junk Mail, and so on. In this case, it would be wise to exclude the Junk Mail folder from being archived.

 You should also look for the ability to include emails in the retention policy for an indefinite period of time. This feature allows you to set a litigation hold, in response to litigation, by simply clicking a "Hold Disposition Process Indefinitely" box.

When setting the actual retention period, you want to be more specific than one-year increments. Archiving solutions should give you the ability to designate days, weeks, months, or years.

Also, it is a good idea to be able to include or exclude different message classes. For example, for those companies with digital phone systems with unified messaging, voicemails attached to emails can be excluded to save storage space.

Email Retention Policy Benefits

The benefits of first developing and then automating your email retention policy are threefold:

- ✔ The first is regulatory compliance. Email retention for regulatory compliance isn't a choice, but rather an absolute requirement. The only choice your company will have is how you meet the requirements: manually or with email archiving automation. Creating and automating your email retention policy lowers your overall risk of noncompliance and ensures all required email is kept for the required time period.

- ✔ The second benefit addresses legal risk management. The ability to show a court an updated and regularly enforced email retention policy can demonstrate retention policy intent and negate claims of spoliation by the plaintiff's attorney.

- ✔ The last obvious benefit relates to document retention for corporate governance. Businesses rely on the generation, use, and reference of data to make ongoing business decisions. The data business generates has a value to the business if that data can be used efficiently.

An effective retention policy ensures that information is available for some period of time and an email archiving system allows for quick search and reference.

Disposition of Email from the Email Archive

Based on the retention time period governed by the email archiving solution, records such as email, attachments, and other objects will be automatically deleted out of the email archive if no litigation hold process is in place. Some archiving solutions automatically hold email that has reached the end of the retention period until someone, usually IT, approves the deletion. As you can imagine, in large systems with millions or billions of emails, this isn't an effective policy.

Chapter 6

eDiscovery and Email Archiving

*Y*our typical employee averaged 142 sent and received emails per day in 2007. The content in these messages was used for improving business communications, enhancing customer satisfaction, and maintaining a competitive edge in today's business environment. (Email can also contain a huge amount of spam, but this book concentrates on the important stuff for now.) This deluge of email communication has created an enormous challenge to businesses that must manage emailed content for *legal discovery* (providing requested data for federal civil lawsuits) and overall corporate governance.

What Is eDiscovery?

eDiscovery (or electronic discovery) refers to the legal process where electronic data is sought, found, reviewed, and produced with the intent of supporting or proving a case by the opposing legal team. All electronic data is subject to the discovery process, which means that email server message stores, email server backup tapes, employee work stations, individual external hard disks, network share drives, PDAs, cell phones, USB thumb drives, removable media such as CD or DVD disks, iPods, digital cameras, and even employee personal email accounts are subject to legal eDiscovery. In all cases, the judge is the final decision maker as to what data is discoverable.

New Amendments to the FRCP

The Federal Rules of Civil Procedure (FRCP) govern court procedures for civil suits in the United States district courts. Although federal courts are required to apply the substantive law of the states as rules of decision in cases where state law is in question, the federal courts almost always use the FRCP as their rules of procedure. States make their own rules that apply in their own courts, but most states have adopted rules that are based on the FRCP.

A number of amendments to the FRCP took effect on December 1, 2006. These new revisions will have a major effect on how companies retain, store, and produce electronic data (including email) for litigation. The new amendments define what electronically stored information (ESI) is, what ESI must be disclosed, and when. They also place new requirements on the parties' knowledge of their own electronic infrastructure — they have to know what ESI they have, where it's stored, how it's retained, and how it's deleted. The FRCP also reiterates the parties' obligations for preserving potential electronic evidence.

These new amendments were created because ESI is normally stored in much greater volume than are hard copy documents. It's also dynamic, and can be modified simply by turning a computer on and off. It can also be incomprehensible when separated from the systems that created it. Finally, ESI contains *metadata*, or information about files and documents, that describes the context of the information and provides other useful and important information.

The changes reflect the reality that discovery of email and other ESI is now a routine but critical aspect of every litigated case. The important things to remember include:

- ✔ The amendments treat ESI differently than conventional records.

- ✔ They require early discussion of and attention to electronic discovery.

> ✔ They address inadvertent production of privileged or protected materials.
>
> ✔ They encourage a two-tiered approach to discovery: deal with reasonably accessible information and then later with inaccessible data.
>
> ✔ They provide a safe harbor from sanctions by imposing a good faith requirement.

Any organization that can be sued in federal court is subject to these new amendments. In effect, this includes everyone, and organizations need to plan all aspects of their electronic infrastructure including litigation hold capability and ESI retention policies.

For specifics on these rules, see the appendix.

The Litigation Hold: Why Should I Care?

A *litigation hold* (or stop destruction notice) is the systematic process, including communications to affected employees, to stop the routine records retention/destruction procedures for records that may be required in an upcoming legal proceeding. A litigation hold applies to all responsive records, documents, files, and emails (both electronic and hardcopy) that exist. In many companies, the email system is the largest repository of responsive records due to the nature of corporate email. Email messages can include business instructions, legal contracts, financial data, presentations, and unguarded opinions about many business-related activities and is therefore a major target of discovery in litigation.

Halting email deletion when legal action is anticipated or actually pending is a legal requirement imposed on all businesses, whether privately or publicly held, by various U.S. legal precedents as well as the FRCP. Failure to stop this destruction can cause charges of *spoliation* (the hiding or destruction of litigation evidence), court sanctions such as fines, and the imposition of an adverse inference instruction by the judge.

Stopping the destruction of email, including calendar entries, contacts, and task lists, because of anticipated or pending litigation is an absolute must and can be very challenging for an organization. Recognizing and planning for litigation holds and discovery can dramatically lower the adverse effects on your employees and lower your overall cost of legal defense.

Other Drivers for eDiscovery and Email Archiving

Another driver for email system eDiscovery is for internal or corporate governance. Corporate governance includes conducting internal investigations for all sorts of reasons, including criminal activity, sexual harassment, enforcing corporate policies, and tracking intellectual property leakage.

Internal investigations for criminal activity

Many companies have to periodically deal with potential criminal activity within their operations, such as drug dealing or identity theft. Another reason for email review is to stop inappropriate behavior such as sexual harassment of employees. In both types of situations, it is the company's responsibility to control the work environment and infrastructure to deal with these kinds of activities. To reduce the company's potential liability, it is a good practice to periodically review (with select auditors) email activity and specific mailbox content to lower the possibility of these activities. It is also a good practice to inform employees that all email content is subject to review by company representatives.

Enforcing corporate policies

It may not be illegal, but using corporate email for personal use ("Hey, I'm selling some football tickets — respond if interested!") can represent a loss of time and resources for the company. A select review of these messages (along with making employees aware of this policy) can reduce the likelihood of this occurrence.

Intellectual property

Another kind of criminal activity many companies deal with is the theft of their intellectual property (IP). IP is easily removed from the company via the corporate email system in the form of attachments. It is difficult to ensure this never happens but IP theft can be stopped by regular reviews of key employee sent items folders.

Part III
The Part of Tens

The 5th Wave   By Rich Tennant

"If I'm not gaining weight, then why does this digital image take up 3MB more memory than a comparable one taken six months ago?"

In this part . . .

The part of tens is a *For Dummies* tradition. In this part, we go over some questions you should probably ask before you start looking for an archiving solution. We also take a look at some great benefits to email archiving. Finally, we've included an informative appendix that goes into detail about the new amendments to the FRCP and major regulatory laws that should affect your email archiving decisions.

Chapter 7

Ten Questions to Ask Yourself Before Shopping for an Email Archiving Solution

Socrates believed that questions helped develop knowledge, and we're not ones to argue (at least not with Socrates). This chapter goes over some questions you should ask yourself while you're kicking the tires on a new archival system.

Always understand why your company is contemplating purchasing an email archiving solution. Asking yourself the questions in this chapter before you purchase a solution will help you better understand what type of solution you really need for your specific circumstances.

What Is the Best Solution for My Company: Hosted or In-House?

A *hosted* email archiving solution means that all of your company email is stored off-site by another company. This solution usually has lower start-up costs and is a little quicker to implement. Because the service provider supplies all the required hardware and software within their facility, you have no upfront equipment or software costs.

However, your hosted email archiving service costs can also be much higher, especially over the long term. Many of these providers price the solution based on the amount of storage your email archive consumes. Remember, these providers have to pay for the software and equipment, so usage and storage costs need to be compared to your expected storage requirements over the life of the archive and the projected service requirements, such as additional costs for accessing the archive and eDiscovery costs.

Many companies are uncomfortable with entrusting another company to store and have access to their corporate communications. You're never entirely sure who has access to your information after it leaves your building and your servers.

An *in-house* email archiving solution refers to the requirement that you purchase the software and hardware and install and manage the solution from within your data centers. The solution and all equipment are owned and managed by you. That means your sensitive corporate data is kept and controlled by your employees in your facilities.

The in-house solution is much more customizable. Because you own and control all aspects of the solution, changes beneficial to your specific requirements are quick to implement and don't require additional service costs. Long-term costs can be noticeably lower due to the fact that the price per gigabyte for storage hardware has shown a marked reduction every year so you're not paying an inflated price.

What Is Scalability, and Do I Need to Worry about It?

Scalability is the ability of the archive to add additional mailboxes, Exchange servers, or additional locations. Scalability usually comes up when a company is growing quickly and wants to add new employee mailboxes to the email archive, or one company acquires another one and wants to add those new employees to their existing email archive. Adding large numbers of new mailboxes or many additional Exchange servers to an already existing email archive can cause serious problems if the email archiving solution isn't able to expand quickly, or the architecture of the email archive won't handle additional strain.

 Look at email archiving solutions with proven architectures that allow for large scalability requirements, such as those solutions built on a grid architecture.

How Long Will I Be Archiving Email?

You've obviously decided you need to retain your corporate email for some amount of time. Otherwise, you wouldn't be asking this question in the first place. Now you need to know how long you should keep the data. The reality is that this is a question that each organization needs to decide by itself. For example, does your company have government regulatory retention requirements, how long is access to old emails productive to your employee, what kind of access does your HR department need for internal governance, and finally, what does your corporate legal department think? Minus regulatory retention requirements, each company will come to its own conclusions.

Do I Need Journaling or Log Shipping Capability?

If you need to capture each and every message without interference from your employees, then you need either journaling or log shipping.

Journaling saves a copy of each email and attachment sent or received and stores the email in a separate Exchange mailbox called the journal mailbox. However, email within this journal mailbox loses all audit and tracking information. For example, you can't determine whether the email message was modified, what folders it resided in, and what happened to the message after it was sent or received. And journaling does not capture deleted emails, drafts, calendar items, task lists, or contacts, all of which are legally discoverable objects within the Exchange system. Of further concern, Microsoft has stated that journaling has a negative performance impact on the Microsoft Exchange Server.

Conversely, *log shipping* uses the standard Exchange transaction log files to capture all Exchange information and has no impact on the performance of an email server. Each transaction log contains a complete set of all Exchange database transactions (such as calendars, contacts, notes, tasks, and so on) that occur, not just sent and received email messages. Well done!

Do I Need to Search the Email Archive to Respond to eDiscovery Requests?

For companies that have been or will be involved in federal civil legal actions, the answer is probably yes. With estimates that over 95 percent of business information is now being produced in electronic form, organizations need to realize that there is no getting around eDiscovery. And a large percentage of discovery requests in federal civil legal actions target the email system where the electronic business information is stored. Because you can't really predict if you'll be in a federal civil legal action (sadly), you should probably be able to search your archive whether you think you'll need it or not.

In federal proceedings, the attorneys ask for hardcopy and electronic records from the defense to help prove their cases. There are claims that approximately 75 percent of U.S. businesses have had to respond to at least one federal discovery request in the last 12 months. This usually entails the defense (maybe your company) reviewing their documents and records for those details requested by the plaintiffs. This can be extremely expensive and time consuming.

In the last few years, corporate email systems have become the first target of eDiscovery orders. Be aware!

Do I Need to Worry about Imposing a Litigation Hold?

The Federal Rules of Civil Procedure (FRCP) require that all parties to an anticipated or real legal proceeding protect all records and data that could be required in the legal proceeding. In the case of your corporate email system, that includes all email, attachments, calendar entries, task lists, and notes within the system that could have a bearing on the case. Those records must be immediately found and protected as potential evidence. The *litigation hold* is the internal process a company uses to find and protect that data. There are harsh penalties if records/data are deleted, even if it's done inadvertently.

When looking at an email archiving solution, the ability to quickly place a litigation hold on specific mailboxes and data is a must.

Do I Give Employees Access to Their Specific Mailbox Archive, and Why?

In most cases the answer is absolutely. By allowing employees access to their archived mailboxes, you increase employee productivity. Your employees no longer have to search through their own PSTs to find old content they want to reference or reuse.

It also frees up your IT staff. Those intrepid workers are no longer dealing with requests to recover old emails from backup tapes — the employees can do these themselves through the archive. Obviously, though, you want your employees to have access to only their own mailboxes for security reasons.

Should I Incorporate PSTs into the Archive?

Whether you can incorporate PSTs into your company email archive depends on several factors. First, have you determined employees are spending measurable time either accessing PSTs looking for old data or is your IT department spending time recovering deleted emails? Most companies find that employees spend approximately two to four hours per week searching for data from old emails and attachments or recreating that data when they can't find the old email. Another factor is how much network storage space PSTs are consuming. Many companies find that their network share drives are clogged with employee PSTs.

Incorporating employee PSTs into a central archive saves storage space because many email archiving solutions create a single instance of each message. Plus, incorporating all emails including those emails in PSTs greatly simplifies discovery of the email system due to the fact that all email related data is located in the archive, not on employee desktops, network drives, or even backup tapes.

How Does an Email Archiving Solution Change My Exchange Server Backup Requirements?

Having an email archiving solution in place doesn't necessarily remove your requirement to backup your email servers. Your Exchange system has many different types of data files that enable it to run effectively. Most email archiving systems capture copies of email messages and attachments, but they don't capture all the other data resident in the server like the Exchange database, calendar data, the contacts database, and tasks and so they can't act as a backup and restore application. Ask the vendor whether its archiving system captures all the data resident in Exchange and whether it provides any backup and restore capability. The standard first-generation email archiving solutions don't capture all the required files to act as a backup and restore application.

Second-generation email archiving solutions that use *log shipping* capture complete mailbox information from Exchange, so they can effectively perform continuous data protection for Exchange and also protect Exchange against disaster.

How Does an Email Archiving Solution Change My Exchange Storage Requirements?

In some cases, your email archival solution can reduce your existing email storage by as much as 80 percent, and it can manage your email storage moving ahead. Now you can manage and control your email storage budget, without sacrificing user productivity.

Keep in mind the email archive can either completely remove email from the email server, or remove and replace it with a small stub file. Both methods will reduce email storage, but the latter potentially introduces thousands of small files that may cause performance problems with Outlook as their numbers increase.

Chapter 8

Ten Major Benefits of Email Archiving

*E*mail archiving can be extremely helpful in today's business environment. There may be no rule of thumb as to when you should buy an email archiving system, but it's a good idea to review the next ten benefits of email archiving and see whether any strike a chord.

Meet Federal or State Regulatory Requirements

Companies in certain industries are required by federal or state law to archive specific records, including email, for specific time periods. Not meeting these retention requirements can have unwanted results — large monetary fines against the company or even individuals, loss of licenses, loss of access to markets, confiscation of goods, or even jail terms. Email archiving solutions were originally developed specifically for regulatory compliance. By installing an email archiving solution that captures and archives that content (email) required by the retention regulations, a company meets its regulatory requirements. For more on this topic, see the appendix.

Respond to eDiscovery Orders and Litigation Hold Requirements

The deluge of email communication has created an enormous challenge to businesses that must manage emailed content for *legal discovery* (providing requested data for federal civil lawsuits) and overall corporate governance. For more on this topic, see Chapter 6.

Increase Your Exchange Server's Performance

As mailboxes and servers become overloaded with content, their performance suffers. It may take longer to open your Outlook client or call up an email to read. Or it may take longer for end-users to conduct searches within their mailboxes. These problems and many more are usually due to excessive content within the Exchange server. Many email archiving solutions include the ability to extend or stub messages and/or their attachments and move (not just copy) them over to the email archive server. This means that the email message from HR with a 1 megabyte PDF attachment is actually replaced on the email server with a *pointer* to the archive. Millions of emails and gigabytes or terabytes of data are removed from the email server while still being available to the end-user. This action removes huge amounts of data from the Exchange server thereby increasing its overall performance.

Reduce Your Exchange Server Backup and Recovery Times

By moving emails and/or attachments off the email server onto the archive server, you have less data to backup or restore. In reality, you're backing up and restoring a large amount of very small pointers instead of full emails and huge attachments. The same holds true when restoring data due to a corrupted mailbox or email server. Some email archiving solutions, those that utilize transaction log shipping, actually capture and keep current the Exchange server's database file, which means these solutions can actually act as the Exchange server backup and restore functionality. This means that you don't have to separately back them up at all. It also provides your company with much better Recovery Point Objectives (RPO) and Recovery Time Objectives (RTO) measures.

Reduce Storage Requirements to Lower Your Overall Storage Costs

Some email archiving solutions create a single instance of each Exchange object. For example, an email and attachment sent to all 1,000 employees in a company from the HR department will be represented by just one message and attachment. This single instance can save huge amounts of storage space.

Increase Employee Productivity

An obvious benefit to an email archiving system is the ability to have unlimited or *supersized* mailboxes. Because employees don't have to adhere to mailbox size limitations, they don't have to spend hours each week moving email to PSTs. Another benefit is that employees search for and recover their own email content. Because emails aren't deleted from the email archive, end-users can search for emails they wish to reuse or reference quickly without spending large amounts of time searching for them in PSTs. This employee self-service also increases IT productivity because IT personnel are no longer spending time recovering deleted email for employees.

Adopt Internal Corporate Governance Processes

Good corporate governance processes can help reduce costs, ensure regulatory compliance, and reduce the risk of outside legal action. Making sure given processes are done in a cost-effective legal manner means creating rules that state why the policies are in place, expectations for meeting the policies by employees, what will happen if the rules aren't followed, and tools to assist meeting the policy expectations. For example, by installing an email archiving solution, you automate email retention to meet regulatory or legal requirements. For more on policies, see Chapter 5.

More Effective Corporate Knowledge Management

Corporate email systems are now the biggest repository of corporate information, intellectual property, and know-how. The problem is that most companies force employees to manage their email separately from the rest of the company. Emails with important corporate information are regularly deleted because employee mailboxes are full and they're instructed to clear some emails out. The deleted emails could have important corporate information not available anywhere else. A central email archive stores, protects, indexes, and retains (per retention policies) all the emails and attachments containing unique data.

Lower Migration Costs

As Microsoft brings out major new revisions to Exchange, many companies eventually migrate from their current revision to the newest. This usually entails moving the entire Exchange database from the earlier version to the latest and greatest. The Exchange database can be extremely large and take a lot of time to move to the newest version. Incorporating an email archive before the migration takes place reduces the size of the Exchange database, meaning there is much less data to migrate to the new version.

Eliminate PSTs

Managing existing PST data is a challenge for companies in regard to legal risk as well as for storage management. These files are usually located on either employee desktops or buried in network drives, and they're difficult to find and manage. The majority of employee desktops aren't protected or backed up, which creates the risk of losing the valuable business emails that reside there.

Email archiving can relieve this situation by migrating all existing employee PSTs into the email archive. This practice ensures lower overall legal risk by enabling central management and protection of PST emails so a litigation hold can be placed and guaranteed quickly as well as lowering the cost of eDiscovery of email data by storing and managing all email data centrally.

PST migration into a central email archive also reduces storage requirements by creating a single instance of each email object thereby eliminating megabytes or gigabytes of copies.

Appendix

The FRCP and Regulatory Drivers for Email Archiving

● ●

*O*dds are very high that your company or firm is subject to some regulation on how you retain records. Some industries may face stricter rules than others (a health care company is probably subject to more rules than a tool-and-die shop), but regulations are something that just about everybody has to deal with.

This appendix goes over some of the laws regarding email retention.

The Sarbanes-Oxley Act (SOX)

Its real name may be "The Public Company Accounting Reform and Investor Protection Act of 2002," but it's better known as the Sarbanes-Oxley Act, and it applies mainly to publicly traded companies. It was passed mostly in response to the front-page news headlines of corporate corruption and financial scandals in recent years, namely Enron and WorldCom. Also known as the "Enron Law," Sarbanes-Oxley provides severe criminal penalties, including prison sentences, for corporate executives who knowingly destroy business documents and other information used in the running of the enterprise. The act also calls out specific records types that need to be retained and requires a records retention period of seven years.

New Amendments to the FRCP

A number of amendments to the Federal Rules of Civil Procedure (FRCP) took effect on December 1, 2006. These new revisions will have a major effect on how companies retain, store, and produce electronic data for litigation.

Rule 16 (b)

This rule is designed to alert the court and litigants to the possible need to address the handling of discovery of ESI (electronically stored information) early in the litigation process. Rule 16(b) is amended to invite the court to address disclosure or discovery of ESI in the Rule 16 scheduling order and gives the court discretion to enter an order adopting any agreements the parties reach for asserting claims of privilege or protection after inadvertent production in discovery.

Rule 26 (a) (1)

The rule clarifies a party's duty to include ESI in its initial disclosures. This amendment also requires the party responding to discovery be able to describe where, in what form, and the accessibility of all ESI they have in their possession. In part, it reads:

> A copy of, or a description by category and location of, all documents, electronically stored information, and tangible things that are in the possession, custody, or control of the party and that the disclosing party may use to support its claims or defenses, unless solely for impeachment.

This rule removes maneuvering room around producing ESI such as instant messages, SMS messages, voicemail, or other forms of electronic data in various locations such as removable storage devices like USB thumb drives, digital camera memory, and iPods. The organization must have a location and inventory of all electronic data ready at the pretrial conference.

Rule 26 (b) (2)

The rule clarifies the obligations of a responding party to provide discovery of ESI that isn't reasonably accessible (deleted information, information kept on some backup tape systems, and legacy data from systems no longer in use). The amendment requires the responding party to identify the sources of potentially responsive information that it hasn't searched or produced because of the costs and burdens of accessing the information. If the requesting party moves for production of such information, the responding party has the burden of showing the information isn't reasonably accessible. If the responding party makes this showing, a court may order discovery for good cause and may impose conditions.

You should first obtain and examine the information that can be provided from easily accessed sources and then determine whether it is necessary to search less accessible sources. A party might be obligated to preserve information stored on sources it has identified as not reasonably accessible. Company representatives, including the corporate legal team, now must be fully knowledgeable of their corporate data infrastructure at the pretrial meeting to discuss the eDiscovery plan.

Rule 26 (b) (5)

This rule provides a procedure for asserting privilege after production. When the providing party claims electronic information may be privileged, the recipient must return, sequester, or destroy the information until the claim is resolved. If, for example, the producing party inadvertently turns over data that is not responsive to the eDiscovery order or is considered privileged and not discoverable, the party in possession must return the data without review.

The producing party must quickly let the receiving party know that they have turned over data they didn't mean to. The receiving party is under no obligation to make a determination on what data is privileged and what data isn't. The receiving party is obligated to return privileged information as soon as possible without reviewing or reading the requested data.

Rule 26 (f)

The rule requires that the parties' pretrial conference include a discussion of issues relating to disclosure or discovery of ESI, including what form or format the discovered data will be produced in (such as paper or electronic form), what data is considered inaccessible and why, and what data is considered privileged.

It also requires businesses to know precisely where all their records are kept, in what format, and how long they're kept in order to negotiate eDiscovery issues at the early meet-and-confer meeting.

Rule 34

This rule explicitly recognizes ESI as a category of discoverable data. Rule 34 also allows the requesting party to specify the form or format of data production, such as a hard paper copy, an electronic PDF file, or the original file format.

Without specific direction from the court or requesting party, the producing party may produce the responsive data in the native or reasonably usable format. A key provision of Rule 34 is the production of data in "a form or forms in which it is ordinarily maintained or in a form or forms that are reasonably usable." This rule allows for an agreement at the initial meet-and-confer meeting between the parties for what form or format the responsive data will be produced. This eliminates the past practice of providing requested ESI in formats difficult to use, such as hundreds of boxes of printed email.

Rule 37 (f)

This rule creates a "safe harbor" that protects the discovered party from adverse sanctions for failing to provide ESI because of inadvertent loss due to "good faith" operation of the company's electronic infrastructure. For example, if the company initiates a litigation hold and takes other measures to preserve all potentially responsive ESI after it is made aware of possible litigation, then the company could claim safe harbor if responsive data is inadvertently lost or deleted. For example, an optical disk could be accidentally scratched in transit, or a hard drive could crash. The key to claiming safe harbor is being able to show the court that your company took several steps to ensure responsive data was not deleted or lost. This proof can take the form of existing data retention policies, formal litigation hold and discovery procedures, and employee awareness campaigns.

SEC Rule 17a-3 and a-4

The U.S. Securities and Exchange Commission (SEC), which regulates financial organizations, has implemented a comprehensive and specific set of rules for the management of electronic communication. These rules were enacted in 1997 to allow brokers and traders in the security industry to store records electronically.

SEC Rule 17 a-3 requires brokers and traders to create and store specific records such as customer communications and customer account trading activities. It also forces brokers and traders to keep those records for a specific period of time on non-rewritable electronic media (WORM) and make them ready for easy review by the SEC within a reasonable time-frame, typically 24 hours.

Health Insurance Portability and Accountability Act (HIPAA)

The HIPAA requirements have been phased in over the last several years and set national standards for the healthcare industry for patient information. Among other things, HIPPA requires that patient records and related data (including related email) must be archived for at least two years after the death of the patient in a secure manner that ensures privacy and content integrity.

Title 21 CFR Part 11

This set of regulations was issued in 1997 by the U.S. Food and Drug Administration (FDA) to establish standards for electronic information and signatures. These are intended to replace hard copies for all manufacturers regulated by the

FDA. It requires that "copies" of all records are kept "in common portable formats" and must preserve the original content and meaning of the records. It also requires the protection of records to enable their accurate and ready retrieval throughout the records retention period. Retention periods include:

- ✔ Food (manufacturing, processing, packing): Two years after release

- ✔ Drugs (manufacturing, processing, packing): Three years after distribution

- ✔ Bio products (manufacturing, processing, packing): Five years after end of manufacturing

ISO 15489 (Worldwide)

The International Organization for Standardization (ISO) has released ISO 15489 - Information and Documentation, Records Management. This standard offers guidelines on the classification, conversion, destruction, disposition, migration, preservation, tracking, and transfer of records.

Federal Acquisition Regulations (FAR) Subpart 4.7 Contractors Records Retention

This regulation provides policies and procedures for retention of records by federal government contractors to meet the records review requirements. All individuals and companies who contract to supply goods or services to the federal government must retain all related records; hardcopy or electronic. It also provides for "timely and convenient access" in the case of an audit, and it applies to both conventional and electronic records.

Title 17 CFR Part 1

This regulation, issued in 1999 by the U.S. Commodity Futures Trading Commission (CFTC), amended the recordkeeping requirements of Commission Regulation 1.3. It allows record keepers for futures trading companies to store information either on electronic media or on micrographic media. This regulation also requires that "record keepers store required records for the full five-year maintenance period" while continuing to provide commission auditors and investigators with timely access to a reliable system of records.

FERC Part 125

The Federal Energy Regulatory Commission (FERC), under the Federal Power Act and Natural Gas Act, sets specific retention periods for the public utilities industry and states the records must have a life expectancy equal to or greater than the specified retention periods.

NARA Part 1234

The National Archives and Records Administration (NARA) regulations specify what government agency records are kept, for how long, and in what form and how they are to be accessed.

Freedom of Information Act (FOIA) — for Federal Agencies

The Freedom of Information Act allows for the full or partial disclosure of previously unreleased information and documents controlled by the U.S. Government. The act, which relies on the NARA regulations mentioned in the previous section, defines federal agency records subject to disclosure, outlines mandatory disclosure procedures, and under certain circumstances, timeframes for response.

The Patriot Act

The Patriot Act requires the Secretary of the Treasury to prescribe regulations "setting forth the minimum standards for financial institutions and their customers regarding the identity of the customer that shall apply in connection with the opening of an account at a financial institution." Broker-dealers must have a fully implemented customer identification program (CIP) that includes procedures for making and maintaining a record of all information obtained.

Federal Employment Related Regulations

There are many federal employment regulations that require some sort of records retention, and they apply to all companies with employees. Some of the better known are:

- Title VII of the Civil Rights Act of 1964
- Age Discrimination in Employment Act
- Americans with Disabilities Act
- Family and Medical Leave Act
- Equal Pay Act of 1963
- Vocational Rehabilitation Act
- Employee Retirement Income Security Act of 1974
- National Labor Relations Act
- Fair Labor Standards Act

The employment regulations are a good sampling of employer requirements, so any company that employs people should at least consider email archiving as a way to meet the above regulations.

The regulatory requirements outlined in the preceding list are the main federal government drivers for records retention including email data, but keep in mind these are not all of them. More than 10,000 records retention regulations are effective in the U.S. Many of these are state-mandated, so a review of the regulations from the states your company operates in would be a great idea.

BUSINESS, CAREERS & PERSONAL FINANCE

0-7645-9847-3

0-7645-2431-3

Also available:
- Business Plans Kit For Dummies 0-7645-9794-9
- Economics For Dummies 0-7645-5726-2
- Grant Writing For Dummies 0-7645-8416-2
- Home Buying For Dummies 0-7645-5331-3
- Managing For Dummies 0-7645-1771-6
- Marketing For Dummies 0-7645-5600-2

- Personal Finance For Dummies 0-7645-2590-5*
- Resumes For Dummies 0-7645-5471-9
- Selling For Dummies 0-7645-5363-1
- Six Sigma For Dummies 0-7645-6798-5
- Small Business Kit For Dummies 0-7645-5984-2
- Starting an eBay Business For Dummies 0-7645-6924-4
- Your Dream Career For Dummies 0-7645-9795-7

HOME & BUSINESS COMPUTER BASICS

0-470-05432-8

0-471-75421-8

Also available:
- Cleaning Windows Vista For Dummies 0-471-78293-9
- Excel 2007 For Dummies 0-470-03737-7
- Mac OS X Tiger For Dummies 0-7645-7675-5
- MacBook For Dummies 0-470-04859-X
- Macs For Dummies 0-470-04849-2
- Office 2007 For Dummies 0-470-00923-3

- Outlook 2007 For Dummies 0-470-03830-6
- PCs For Dummies 0-7645-8958-X
- Salesforce.com For Dummies 0-470-04893-X
- Upgrading & Fixing Laptops For Dummies 0-7645-8959-8
- Word 2007 For Dummies 0-470-03658-3
- Quicken 2007 For Dummies 0-470-04600-7

FOOD, HOME, GARDEN, HOBBIES, MUSIC & PETS

0-7645-8404-9

0-7645-9904-6

Also available:
- Candy Making For Dummies 0-7645-9734-5
- Card Games For Dummies 0-7645-9910-0
- Crocheting For Dummies 0-7645-4151-X
- Dog Training For Dummies 0-7645-8418-9
- Healthy Carb Cookbook For Dummies 0-7645-8476-6

- Home Maintenance For Dummies 0-7645-5215-5
- Horses For Dummies 0-7645-9797-3
- Jewelry Making & Beading For Dummies 0-7645-2571-9
- Orchids For Dummies 0-7645-6759-4
- Puppies For Dummies 0-7645-5255-4
- Rock Guitar For Dummies 0-7645-5356-9
- Sewing For Dummies 0-7645-6847-7
- Singing For Dummies 0-7645-2475-5

INTERNET & DIGITAL MEDIA

0-470-04529-9

0-470-04894-8

Also available:
- Blogging For Dummies 0-471-77084-1
- Digital Photography For Dummies 0-7645-9802-3
- Digital Photography All-in-One Desk Reference For Dummies 0-470-03743-1
- Digital SLR Cameras and Photography For Dummies 0-7645-9803-1
- eBay Business All-in-One Desk Reference For Dummies 0-7645-8438-3

- HDTV For Dummies 0-470-09673-X
- Home Entertainment PCs For Dummies 0-470-05523-5
- MySpace For Dummies 0-470-09529-6
- Search Engine Optimization For Dummies 0-471-97998-8
- Skype For Dummies 0-470-04891-3
- The Internet For Dummies 0-7645-8996-2
- Wiring Your Digital Home For Dummies 0-471-91830-X

---

* Separate Canadian edition also available
† Separate U.K. edition also available

Available wherever books are sold. For more information or to order direct: U.S. customers visit www.dummies.com or call 1-877-762-2974.
U.K. customers visit www.wileyeurope.com or call 0800 243407. Canadian customers visit www.wiley.ca or call 1-800-567-4797.

SPORTS, FITNESS, PARENTING, RELIGION & SPIRITUALITY

0-471-76871-5

0-7645-7841-3

Also available:
- Catholicism For Dummies 0-7645-5391-7
- Exercise Balls For Dummies 0-7645-5623-1
- Fitness For Dummies 0-7645-7851-0
- Football For Dummies 0-7645-3936-1
- Judaism For Dummies 0-7645-5299-6
- Potty Training For Dummies 0-7645-5417-4

- Buddhism For Dummies 0-7645-5359-3
- Pregnancy For Dummies 0-7645-4483-7 †
- Ten Minute Tone-Ups For Dummies 0-7645-7207-5
- NASCAR For Dummies 0-7645-7681-X
- Religion For Dummies 0-7645-5264-3
- Soccer For Dummies 0-7645-5229-5
- Women in the Bible For Dummies 0-7645-8475-8

TRAVEL

0-7645-7749-2

0-7645-6945-7

Also available:
- Alaska For Dummies 0-7645-7746-8
- Cruise Vacations For Dummies 0-7645-6941-4
- England For Dummies 0-7645-4276-1
- Europe For Dummies 0-7645-7529-5
- Germany For Dummies 0-7645-7823-5
- Hawaii For Dummies 0-7645-7402-7

- Italy For Dummies 0-7645-7386-1
- Las Vegas For Dummies 0-7645-7382-9
- London For Dummies 0-7645-4277-X
- Paris For Dummies 0-7645-7630-5
- RV Vacations For Dummies 0-7645-4442-X
- Walt Disney World & Orlando For Dummies 0-7645-9660-8

GRAPHICS, DESIGN & WEB DEVELOPMENT

0-7645-8815-X

0-7645-9571-7

Also available:
- 3D Game Animation For Dummies 0-7645-8789-7
- AutoCAD 2006 For Dummies 0-7645-8925-3
- Building a Web Site For Dummies 0-7645-7144-3
- Creating Web Pages For Dummies 0-470-08030-2
- Creating Web Pages All-in-One Desk Reference For Dummies 0-7645-4345-8
- Dreamweaver 8 For Dummies 0-7645-9649-7

- InDesign CS2 For Dummies 0-7645-9572-5
- Macromedia Flash 8 For Dummies 0-7645-9691-8
- Photoshop CS2 and Digital Photography For Dummies 0-7645-9580-6
- Photoshop Elements 4 For Dummies 0-471-77483-9
- Syndicating Web Sites with RSS Feeds For Dummies 0-7645-8848-6
- Yahoo! SiteBuilder For Dummies 0-7645-9800-7

NETWORKING, SECURITY, PROGRAMMING & DATABASES

0-7645-7728-X

0-471-74940-0

Also available:
- Access 2007 For Dummies 0-470-04612-0
- ASP.NET 2 For Dummies 0-7645-7907-X
- C# 2005 For Dummies 0-7645-9704-3
- Hacking For Dummies 0-470-05235-X
- Hacking Wireless Networks For Dummies 0-7645-9730-2
- Java For Dummies 0-470-08716-1

- Microsoft SQL Server 2005 For Dummies 0-7645-7755-7
- Networking All-in-One Desk Reference For Dummies 0-7645-9939-9
- Preventing Identity Theft For Dummies 0-7645-7336-5
- Telecom For Dummies 0-471-77085-X
- Visual Studio 2005 All-in-One Desk Reference For Dummies 0-7645-9775-2
- XML For Dummies 0-7645-8845-1

Are You Struggling to Keep Up With Email Management?
It's Time to Lower Costs, Minimize Risk, Take Control!

With the explosion of user-driven information and the ever-increasing demands of legal discovery, chances are that your organization is struggling to keep up with email management.

- Would you like to reduce your Exchange storage by 50 to 60 percent?
- Are HR-related requests to search email on backup tapes your worst nightmare?
- Is litigation readiness a concern to your business?

If you answered yes to any of these questions, you are not alone.

- Storage requirements will grow from almost 18 MB per user/day in 2007, to over 28 MB per user/day in 2011 (Radicati Group)
- 75% of a company's Intellectual Property is now contained in email (ESG)
- 87% of U.S. corporations are in active litigation (Fulbright & Jaworski L.L.P.)

// I was captivated by Mimosa NearPoint the first time I saw it. It is so simple to use and it fits perfectly in our initiative to empower our users with more self-service capability to manage email. The optimization of our email environment with Mimosa NearPoint helps Virtua Health enhance the quality of patient care, improve clinical safety, meet regulatory requirements, reduce costs, and enhance employee productivity.

—Tom Pacek
AVP of Technology, Virtua Health

Mimosa™ NearPoint™ for Microsoft® Exchange
Comprehensive Email Archiving, Recovery, and Storage Management

Mimosa NearPoint for Microsoft Exchange combines the lowest total cost of ownership with the most scalable email archiving solution on the market. It is the only email archiving solution to integrate email archival, eDiscovery, disaster recovery, and storage management into a single, modular solution.

NearPoint includes a number of features —zero footprint on Exchange, optional agents on desktops, plug-and-play installation, and zero requirement for rearchitecting the production email system—that make it the easiest system to deploy.

But don't let ease of installation fool you. NearPoint is also the most comprehensive solution, going beyond basic email archival to enable recovery and discovery of every aspect of a mailbox—including public folders, offline PST files, calendars, contacts, notes, and more.

(Continued on next page)

(Continued from previous page)

Take Control of Exploding Email Requirements with Email Archiving

Mimosa NearPoint eDiscovery Option
Powerful Search, Retrieval, and Management of Email Assets

The Mimosa™ NearPoint™ eDiscovery Option minimizes legal risks by extending the search capability that is inherent in Mimosa NearPoint to ensure that all Exchange data is made available for quick discovery-based searches. Email assets are protected during litigation with message-level litigation holds that reduce the risk of penalties and fines for spoliation. Access to mailbox content is complete, including all email and recipients (To, From, Cc, Bcc) and all Exchange items (email, calendars, contacts, etc.). Even complex conversation threads can be reconstructed for litigation support and investigations.

Mimosa NearPoint PST Archiving Option
Automated Management of Microsoft Outlook PST Files

Users routinely offload email messages and attachments from Exchange Server to local PST files to stay below mailbox quota limits. However, storing valuable company intellectual property in files that are distributed widely across the enterprise in share drive or employee desktops/laptops presents a significant risk for the organization. The Mimosa NearPoint PST Archiving Option minimizes this risk by automatically locating PST files and actively importing them into the NearPoint archive. And, if you want to eliminate the use of PST files altogether, this option can make that a reality.

Mimosa NearPoint Disaster Recovery Option
Automated Disaster Protection and Service Recovery for Exchange

Mimosa NearPoint enables you to restore Exchange databases, Storage Groups, or the entire Exchange Server in the event of a hardware or software failure. The Disaster Recovery Option extends this capability by enabling restoration of Exchange data to a standby Exchange Server, including restarting of Exchange services and remapping of mailboxes in an Active Directory Server. When disaster strikes, one click is all it takes to initiate complete Exchange failover, providing business continuity of critical Exchange services.

Mimosa Systems
The Leader in Live Content Archiving Solutions

Mimosa Systems delivers next-generation information management solutions for information immediacy, discovery, and continuity. Mimosa is a Microsoft Gold Certified Partner, recognized for competencies in networking infrastructure solutions, ISV/software solutions, and advanced infrastructure solutions. Based in Santa Clara, California, Mimosa has customers around the globe.

 MIMOSA™
SYSTEMS

3200 Coronado Drive
Santa Clara, CA 95054
TEL 408-970-9070
www.mimosasystems.com/nextstep